DIY BIOCHAR IN SMALL BATCHES

UK Pyrolysis, Black Soil Magic and Compost

By James Trebor

RJS Publishing

ISBN-13: 9781912682102 Kindle copy
ISBN-13: 9781912682133 Paperback

Cover design by: RJS

Printed in the UK

CONTENTS

INTRODUCTION

The Brilliance of Black Soil Magic... biochar.

*This book provides information, illustration and instructions on, how and why I produce my Black Soil Magic (biochar) in small batches for addition to the compost heap and use as a soil amendment on my UK allotment.

"I have recently been made to realise that if us gardeners, allotment holders, horticulturalists and agriculturists treated some or all of their organic waste differently, we could help reduce climate change while also benefitting the cultivation of plants on our own piece of land, however small."

The above statement may seem profound, but it is accurate, and, while the individual impact of following such advice may seem globally insignificant, the level of contribution will increase with each of us that embrace a switch.

The main change required is fairly simple. We should swap the burning of biomass into ash with pyrolysis, which makes a char end product. After biological activation, this char becomes Black Soil Magic (a nutrient and microbe packed biochar), providing a fantastically positive soil amendment that can be put to many good uses.

Pyrolysis is the thermal decomposition of any

organic material (plant or animal) in an oxygen-depleted environment to form raw char, but what is biochar, how can we make it with simple methods, and what are the benefits for plant cultivation and the environment?

The raw char that becomes biochar (after being charged with nutrients and inoculated with microbes), is a carbon-rich solid with a vast, sponge-like surface area and high cation exchange capacity. The biochar, which I prefer to call Black Soil Magic (BSM) because of its magical properties, will improve most growth mediums (soil and compost) when added as an amendment, while simultaneously capturing carbon and reducing CO2 release into the environment.

How do we maximise a char end product from a fire instead of ash?

Regular bonfires in the garden, allotment, or smallholding are historically the main way to degrade bulky organic matter into a manageable pile of ash. However, with a few simple changes, the proportion of feedstock that ends up fully combusted could be reduced and the amount pyrolysed to create char, increased.

Reducing combustion

A triangle helps visualise the combustion process. Along the base is organic matter, which we can call feedstock. The two sides of the triangle represent heat and oxygen, the other essential ingredients that, together with feedstock, create combustion and associated flames producing heat to release gases and yield an ash end product.

During this irreversible process, oxygen atoms bind with carbon atoms to form CO2, a colourless gas. An imbalance in the amount of CO2 released into the atmosphere compared to that used up (by plant respiration, etc.) can negatively impact climate change.

Increasing the proportion of Pyrolised biomass

For pyrolysis to occur, heat must decompose part of the feedstock to form an almost pure carbon char instead of ash. The combustion process will fail to be completed when there are insufficient oxygen molecules to bond with carbon molecules (achieved by creating a reduced oxygen environment).

You can make raw char on either a large or small scale, but this book concentrates on small batches of up to one hundred litres of finished product at a time, made using simple, readily available garden equipment. To achieve a given finished amount of char, around five times that volume of feedstock must be decomposed, plus additional feedstock burned in the presence of oxygen to create adequate flaming heat for the process.

Two simple ways of achieving a good level of pyrolysis are particularly suited to small-batch production.

In the first method, a standard fire, burning secondary feedstock, heats a kiln or retort filled with a primary feedstock meant for pyrolysis. The kiln or retort is partially sealed to prevent oxygen entry while allowing gases to escape during decomposition of the biomass. The volatile gases released, including methane, should be burned off by surrounding flames generated by the fire, creating additional heat which helps the pyrolysis process and prevents the release of greenhouse gases like methane into the atmosphere.

The second method operates with an open firepit that, by design, has a restricted oxygen supply to its lower portion. Pyrolysis forms the char in this area, while burning of secondary feedstocks in the top part of the fire creates enough heat for the pyrolysis to occur. Once pyrolysis has occurred in the lower part of the firepit, it is possible to stop adding feedstock to the top section and after full charring of this has happened, quench the entire fire to prevent further combustion of the feedstocks into ash. This will leave char with some ash mixed in.

With either method, the smoke released can also be condensed using a hood and cooling tubes to create wood vinegar, a valuable by-product.

Feedstocks

Primary feedstocks suitable for filling kilns in the

first method must be small enough to fit into the vessels used. Woodchips, dried weeds, or bean pods are good examples.

Secondary feedstocks can be larger, only needing to fit into or overhang the firepit, which saves a lot of effort, cutting up. Char yields will be lower from secondary feedstocks than with the same quantity of primary feedstock because part of the secondary feedstock is combusted into ash out of a necessity to provide the heat for pyrolysis in the oxygen-depleted lower part of the firepit (or in a kiln or retort placed in the fire).

Having set out to create a firepit in which we purposely restrict the oxygen supply to the lower part, the feedstock in that portion will undergo pyrolysis to become inert char. The char has properties depending on the original feedstock, the temperature achieved, and the timescale under which the feedstock was decomposed. The raw char formed will primarily be captured carbon (which, once made, will not break down further, releasing CO_2, unless re-burned).

When the end use for your char is soil amendment, the feedstocks are best pyrolysed at temperatures between 250 and about 700 degrees Celsius (much hotter than charcoal for fuel production). The intense heat breaks down long-chain molecules like lignin and cellulose within plants to create individual molecules, creating a large surface area and **sponge-like characteristics.** These end properties (of char) are particularly helpful in plant cultivation because of the char's ability to absorb nutrients, oxygen or water and provide spaces for microbes to thrive.

Once charged or activated with said ingredients, either in a concentrated form (weed fertiliser, artificial fertiliser, or by addition to a compost heap), I call the product Black Soil Magic (BSM).

BSM biochar can be added to a growth medium, where it will enhance the natural soil biome (community) and promote regenerative connectivity between nutrients, microbes, fungi, and plant roots into the future. Adding Black Soil Magic (BSM Biochar) is particularly effective in poorly structured and acidic soils, where leaching and runoff can be reduced considerably and the PH raised (BSM biochar is most often alkaline). In the modern world, with rapid climate change leading to regular flooding, the sponge-like attribute of horticultural char is particularly beneficial.

Mixing Char and Compost

Crushed char is the perfect companion for home made compost. The carbon solids help activate and maintain the decay of organic matter while the massive surface area around and between char molecules provides a fabulous home for air, water, nutrients and microbes as the char granules become fully charged, forming Black Soil Magic. Although each individual product (either compost or BSM) acts as an excellent soil amendment, I prefer mixing the two before application to garden, allotments or horticultural land.

For this reason, my book explains both the process of composting and of pyrolysis, as well as discussing the mixing ratios, particle size, etc. that I have found to be ideal. All of this is open to your further experimentation.

Before we start, I have prepared a glossary to clarify the words and processes that I came across while researching and creating DIY, small scale, Black Soil Magic (BSM).

GLOSSARY

Allotment: A plot of land for growing vegetables or flowers, rented privately or available from the town or district Council, here in the UK.

Biomass: Organic matter, which can be used as a feedstock for Biochar production or as a compost ingredient.

Bio-active char (Biochar): The name commonly given to organic biomass after undergoing a two-stage process. Firstly, pyrolysis, during which it is heated at a high temperature(250-700+ degrees Celsius) in the presence of little or no oxygen until decomposed. The inert carbon skeleton (char) produced by pyrolysis will remain stable for hundreds of years and becomes BSM biochar (a beneficial soil amendment) after you inoculate the raw char with microbes and nutrients.

Raw char has a large surface area and high cation exchange capacity, which, attracts and stores soil nutrients, water and air, making them available to plants. Adding BSM Biochar also enhances the soil biome, providing a home for beneficial fungi and microbes, and acting like a rechargeable battery, which can be repeatedly re-filled when empty. As a result, nutrient leaching and runoff are reduced, especially in poor soils, and PH increases. As an alternative to burning a biomass source to ashes, producing char by pyrolysis leads to sequestered (captured) carbon, reducing greenhouse gas emissions.

Black Soil Magic (BSM): A descriptive name used in association with or as an alternative to biochar.

Biome: The naturally occurring community of flora and fauna occupying a habitat, e.g. the soil.

Cation Exchange Capacity (CEC): Soil mineral particles and organic matter are mostly negatively charged (called anions) and attract positively charged molecules (called cations), such as nutrients and water. Soil particles with low surface area (for example, sand particles) have a low CEC and possess fewer molecules to attract nutrients (cations). Silt, clay and organic matter particles have increasingly high CEC values (due to their larger surface area). By improving the overall CEC of soil, more nutrient molecules will be bound to the constituent soil particles, thus making them available to plants, and those nutrients will be less likely to leach away. BSM biochar has a very large surface area and high CEC.

Char: Organic biomass that has been pyrolysed (decomposed) at around 250-700 degrees centigrade), Before being nutrified/inoculated to become BSM biochar.

Charcoal: Pyrolysed biomass created at temperatures around 200-300 degrees Celsius.

Charcoal is heavier and denser than char or BSM biochar, retains more aromatic components and has a lower surface area thus it is less suitable as a soil amendment, but is excellent for barbeques, adding aromatic flavours to cooked food.

Raw char with plant xylem and phloem intact.

Flame curtain: A curtain of flames maintained around the point of combustible gas release from any retort (kiln) to ensure those gases (e.g. methane) are burned off and not released into the atmosphere.

Flexi-Kiln: A U-shaped stainless steel, flexible tube that can be pre-filled with biomass feedstock (woodchips, sticks, weeds, etc.) and placed within a burning firepit. Both open ends point upward and are capped with soil to reduce oxygen entry into the tube, allowing combustible gases to burn as they escape from the decomposing feedstock.

Humus: A beneficial, organic constituent of soil. Usually comprising decayed plants or animal parts, it has a high CEC (ability to attract and hold onto nutrients in the soil, making them available to plants in the root zone). BSM biochar is a humus-like organic soil constituent because, after decomposition by heat, it also has a high CEC, which is retained over a long period and, when charged with nutrients, has beneficial effects on the soil biome, aiding plant growth.

Hydrophobic: Hydrophobic molecules repel water. For example, a dry hanging basket can be difficult to water without excessive runoff (or through). This is because compost or soil is hydrophobic when dry, made worse by dense root mass conditions. BSM Biochar can be hydrophobic when freshly made, but once in contact with soil, its surface gradually oxidises, increasing hydrophilicity.

Hydrophilic: Hydrophilic molecules can attract, mix, or dissolve in water.Leaching: The draining or washing through the soil of nutrients or chemicals. Nutrients and chemicals are applied to our crops in varying forms and quantities, but there is a risk of wastage by leaching, especially during heavy rain. Leaching can lead to the contamination of lakes and rivers. The potential for leaching is worst in sandy soils due to their lack of structure and low CEC (ability to hold the nutrients).

Primary Feedstock: Organic matter chopped small enough to fill a Flexi-Tube (or other kiln/retorts), which can be suspended in or over a heat source for pyrolysis, converting the feedstock into char.

Pyrolysis: The decomposition of organic biomass under high temperatures, occurring in a reduced oxygen environment.

Pyrolysing firepit (DIY version): A bottomless steel drum (or similar) placed over a tapered hole dug in the ground. A biomass feedstock is decomposed by heat under reduced oxygen conditions in the lower part of the firepit, converting that portion to char. At the same time, higher up in the fire, the feedstock burns with fierce flames, which use up the available oxygen and create ash. Flexi-Tube kilns (or similar) may be placed in or over the fire so that their contents (primary feedstock) will be decomposed by pyrolysis, creating additional raw char.

A bottomless steel ring, set over a tapered ground pit

Retort or kiln: A vessel, usually made of steel, containing a primary feedstock for thermal decomposition by pyrolysis close to a heat source (fire). DIY vessels include old paint tins or baked bean cans, which are pushed together and should be pierced to allow decomposition gases to escape.

Secondary Feedstock: The organic matter added to an open firepit for heating the flexi tube/kilns. As the secondary feedstock disintegrates, the bits that drop into the lower area of the firepit, where the oxygen supply is depleted, may become char.

Terra Preta: A rich black soil found in the Amazon. It was historically created during deforestation by the slash-and-char process in which char was dug into the soil. Char has a large surface area and high cation exchange capacity for attracting and retaining nutrients and moisture. This reduces leaching. Production of char also captures carbon (sequestration), lessening greenhouse gas emissions.

WeedChar: A name given to char after infusing it with a water-rotted or fermented weed liquid containing nutrients and microbes.

THE HISTORY OF BIOCHAR

The creation and use of Black Soil Magic biochar as a sponge-like amendment to soil is new in the limelight due to its additional capability to reduce global warming. However, biochar production derives from ancient practices in the Amazon rainforest. Here, farmers modified their formerly poor soils, creating richly fertile, black loam known as terra preta. Instead of slashing and burning vegetation during the clearing of woodland for farming, terra preta involved a controlled burn in a trench. By restricting the oxygen supply, some of the biomass was decomposed into char under intense heat, without burning fully (which would have left only ash).

The almost pure carbon char possessed valuable properties. When crumbled into the soil, it held air, water, and nutrients, enhancing microbial and fungal action due to its chemical structure, which has benefitted plants ever since. An associated reduction in nutrient leaching under heavy rain conditions and the fact that biochar is usually alkaline meant acidity was neutralised, and nutrients made more available to plants. These positive biochar effects, stabilised the soil and continued to do so, with minimal char degradation over the centuries since then.

Raw Biochar is almost pure carbon and is

essentially inert. For use as a soil amendment in the garden, allotment, or small-holding, the raw char is best crushed and then activated by inoculating with microbes and charging with nutrients. This can be done by adding a liquid fertiliser or mixing the char with nutrient-rich compost, or both, to create activated Biochar (Black Soil Magic). Once activated and in situ, the biochar supplies nutrients to your growing plants and can be refilled like a rechargeable battery with more nutrients, ready for further distribution throughout the soil biome which makes them available for further uptake by your plants.

In our modern, environmentally conscious world, the positive horticultural, agricultural and environmental implications of making biochar have rapidly expanded its popularity. It has received added kudos because the creation of char from organic matter is now known to capture and remove carbon from the carbon cycle, thereby reducing CO2 and methane emissions into the atmosphere.

Warning: Before attempting pyrolysis, safety considerations and rules must be considered, applied, and adhered to. This is because of the danger of exposure to temperatures exceeding one thousand degrees Celsius and the use of dangerous equipment. Pyrolysis should only be attempted by competent persons over the age of eighteen.

A firepit showing pyrolysis and combustion

CHAPTER 1 PYROLYSIS FEEDSTOCKS

With DIY, small batch biochar production, there are two sizes of feedstock suitable for making the raw char. Primary feedstocks need to be small enough to fit into whatever sized kiln you use, whereas secondary feedstocks are for addition to the open firepit and may be any size that can be burned in the available space. Air drying the feedstocks as much as possible before pyrolysis is crucial for wasting less heat on this process within the fire. Dryness can be measured by the white smoke (mostly moisture) emitted from the firepit.

Secondary feedstock, like logs, wood prunings, brambles, dead weeds, brassica stalks, old bean plants, animal manures, or animal carcasses, are all good, but it is best to match sizes and density for a given production cycle. Add each sized group in a way that will ensure even and complete pyrolysis. After getting the fire started in the usual way, larger diameter pieces are placed on earlier to give them plenty of time to thoroughly thermally decompose.

Gathered leaves, woodchips, bean pods, and twigs provide potential primary feedstocks. These must be small enough to fit inside kilns or retorts (if used). Any feedstock inside the tubes will be converted to almost pure carbon with no ash content because there should be virtually no oxygen inside the kiln, so pack the kiln or retort nice and full.

Before lighting the fire, assemble your range of feedstock sizes and types nearby. This is because a constant fuel supply is necessary to keep the fire burning intensely and to maintain the high temperatures required for thermal decomposition. Various types and sizes of feedstock will be needed to keep plenty of flames at the top of the pit, using up the available oxygen so that oxygen-depleted , thermal decomposition can occur lower down in the firepit. When siting the feedstocks, they need to be near, but not close enough to risk the spread of fire from the firepit.

Woodchip feedstock for stuffing Flexi-Tubes.

The secondary feedstock will be partially burned to ash, creating the heat for the whole process, however, it should also yield a good proportion of BSM biochar as it breaks up and burning embers drop in the oxygen-depleted lower area of the fire.

Secondary feedstocks, rose thorns, fruit tree prunings and dry sweetcorn plants.

CHAPTER 2 MAKING
A DIY FIREPIT

The first thing you need to construct for DIY small batch char production at home, on the allotment or on a smallholding is a fireproof enclosure with no air holes at the base. In its most basic form, this could just be a tapered (inwards as you go deeper) hole in the ground, but most people will be able to get hold of a bottomless steel drum or other fireproof housing to extend the firepit, which is ideal (preferably cut the bottom out, but a standard drum may be used with no holes in the base). I find that the drum doesn't want to be over about three feet high for ease of loading and unloading.

My 700mm diameter drum is made from an old water tank; however, a standard forty-gallon drum cut in half will do the job on a slightly smaller scale. A heat-proof or lined brick enclosure, built with mortar to stop any air from being sucked in through the walls during the burning process is another alternative.

On a slightly larger scale, I also have a 900mm diameter drum. A second, bottomless steel kiln may optionally be positioned inside and this may be filled with wood before a steel lid is fitted over the top.

Alternatively the kiln may be capped with soil or the entire separator can be filled with soil or compost for sterilisation.

Larger firepit with kiln inside (must be capped)

Whatever you choose, remember. the reason for the unusual fire setup is to restrict oxygen availability so that raw char output can be maximised within the firepit area, (which is where the bulk of your feedstock will be added). It is inefficient to only produce char in a sealed kiln/retort heated over the fire.

A decent proportion of char may be harvested direct from the firepit and the open process is easier to manage, but adding one or two Flexi-kilns (or other retorts) containing finer feedstocks into the firepit when it is burning fiercely is worth the extra effort. Not only do the added kilns produce good char, but they help control the burn in the main firepit.

As for my favourite overall setup, I dig a small pit AND, above that, add a cut-off drum (about three feet in height and 700mm-900mm in diameter). My Flexi-Tube kilns/retorts are inserted and heated by the fire, whenever I have small sized feedstocks to make into char and/or for soil sterilisation to make my own compost mix.

The beauty of the bottomless ring over a hole in the ground is that production is increased, wear and tear minimised and the movement, filling and emptying made easier.

CHAPTER 3 DIY KILNS AND RETORTS

My Flexi-Tubes are simple offcuts from stainless steel chimney liners (ask your local wood stove fitter). These can be sprung into a horseshoe shape, gripping the inside edge of the drum, where they are held in position over the flames. To stop the fire from spreading inside the Flexi-Tubes, I cap them with soil at each end. This lets gases escape but minimises oxygen admittance. As a bonus, the soil becomes sterilised in the firepit and may be used to make potting mixes afterwards.

If Flexi-Tube offcuts are unavailable, DIY kilns can

be made from two baked bean cans with their tops snipped so they may be pushed together, one inside the other. Any other old tins with a lid will also do, but remember to pierce the can in a couple of places to allow gases to escape during the decomposition of the feedstock.

I am sure there are many other suitable vessels such as old milk churns or steel buckets that may be worth a try. My opinion is to use whatever is freely available, experimenting to see how long it lasts(heat degradation) and bear in mind how difficult it was to convert into a useful retort or kiln. As a result of my own findings, a preference to cap with soil makes using everyday objects easier because shaping a suitable lid is usually the tricky bit.

CHAPTER 4 TOOLS AND SAFETY.

It is essential to source the right safety equipment before you start.

A sturdy, heat-proof pair of gauntlets, at least one good garden fork, and a steel bar for stirring the char are all necessary when conducting pyrolysis, along with appropriate safety clothing and eye protection. The temperatures reached can easily top one thousand degrees, so sensible positioning of the firepit must be considered, as well as the weather conditions.

Children must be kept away from the entire process for obvious safety reasons. Fire extinguishing tools and an adequate nearby water supply are prerequisites when manufacturing char.

Although biochar may be created in any weather, it is best to do it when the ambient temperature is high and in low wind conditions. This makes the maintenance of over 300 degrees Celsius easier. A useful tool to help with this is a removable lid reflecting the heat inwardly to the firepit. I use the top from a steel drum, laid loosely onto the fire, over, or between the retorts whenever the fire rages. It is easily removed (wearing heat-proof gloves) to refuel. The lid or lids are also helpful at the end of the process for keeping steam within the firepit after adding a small amount of water. Steaming the char helps with its porosity.

Another item I have found essential is a digital/laser thermometer for the firepit (I also use it for greenhouse measurements). A PH monitor and a soil nutrient testing kit are helpful in gardening terms because, when adding BSM biochar as an amendment, it is always worth knowing the soil you are working with to begin with, rather than guessing. Too much alkalinity could have a detrimental effect on nutrient uptake, which over-rides the benefits of the BSM biochar.

CHAPTER 5   WOOD VINEGAR

Wood vinegar is made from the condensed smoke emitted from a BSM biochar production unit. The liquid formed, comprising acetone, acetic acid and methanol, is also known as pyroligneous acid. Because BSM biochar is usually alkaline, one use of collected wood vinegar may be to balance the PH of a char product.

To collect the smoke, you first need a suitable canopy over the firepit, leading to a piped outlet, inside which the smoke can cool condense and drip into a collection vessel. You will end up with brownish wood vinegar and other deposits like tar.

The vinegar is a beneficial by product of biochar production. It can be used in the garden to deal with pests (deter slugs, aphids, etc), invigorate plant growth, and reduce PH levels. The concentrate should be diluted two hundred to one and applied as a foliar spray or direct soil treatment. Alternatively, the mixture can be made twice as strong and added to the compost heap. There are other uses for wood vinegar, which may be researched online. Below is an illustration of a canopy for condensing smoke from your fire, made from an old wheelbarrow and a piece of Flexi-Tube.

CHAPTER 6 LIGHTING THE FIRE

To start things off, a small fire should be lit at the base of the pit with thin sticks.

This can be increased by adding a slightly larger diameter secondary feedstock once white ash has started to form on the first few sticks.

Repeat until a good-sized fire burns, with flames swirling in the top part of the pit or drum. Any charred and broken feedstock will drop down during the burn into the lower, oxygen-depleted area to create a good stock of heat creating embers. You can add some thicker wood to the ember pile as it will take quite a while to pyrolyse.

The fierce, high-level fire will continue to use up the available oxygen and as none can be sucked in from below, the bottom part of the drum will begin creating biochar due to the intense heat from above and below. Keep increasing the fire in the same way whenever the previous feedstock collapses or when you see ash forming on the feedstock.

Some texts advocate starting the fire at the top of a pile of feedstock and letting it back-burn, down into the firepit. My opinion is that heat rises, so starting at the bottom is better, but you can experiment with both methods.

CHAPTER 7 FEEDING THE FIRE

Any secondary feedstock can be poked vertically or at an angle into the firepit, and more should be laid across the top of the drum. It doesn't matter if the secondary feedstock overlaps the drum; just turn it inwards with a fork when the middle of the sticks burn through, allowing them to be broken.

As soon as ash appears on the secondary feedstock, add more dry material, and when this collapses inside, check for an even spread of heat around the drum, stirring if necessary.

If you intend to introduce Flexi-Tubes filled with primary feedstock, do it and then carry on adding to the fire around them. Try to maintain a high and even temperature. I usually aim for the outside of any retort to register over 500 degrees Celsius and the outside of the steel firepit should be about three hundred degrees. It is possible to insulate the firepit walls by building up soil around the outside of the firepit. This helps maintain an even temperature and is especially useful on cold days.

Continue with the above process until all of your feedstock is used up, but steam and then remove the kilns from the fire if you suspect they may have finished (offgas flames have stopped burning and temperature has been consistently high for at least half an hour). The soil caps will also have shrunk down the tubes.

CHAPTER 8 OPEN PIT PYROLYSIS

The stages will be very rapid with open pit pyrolysis when using dry feedstock. Initially, white smoke appears as moisture evaporates (see previous illustration), then yellowy smoke is followed by darker grey or blue smoke as the volatiles within the feedstock are released. In the end, there will be virtually no smoke. Of course, as you add more stock, the smoking sequence will be repeated at the top of the firepit, while the char below should be glowing gently in the oxygen-depleted atmosphere.

After adding most of your feedstock and allowing it to decompose or burn, the drum may be over half full of raw char. At this point, my final feedstocks are added to the open pit. These will be the thinnest of the gathered batch, for example, couch grass and dried bindweed roots (if there is no room for these in a Flexi-Tube or kiln). Thin, dry organic matter will be pyrolysed extremely quickly, so you have to be careful not to turn this stock entirely to ash. I usually add a lot at once to subdue the flames so the inherent heat from below can pyrolyse the weeds without combustion. There is something special in the thought that former noxious and invasive weeds can be converted into valuable soil amendments.

Brambles and nettle roots are my other favourite weeds to burn in an open firepit. After these thinner feedstocks stop smoking, I lay the two flat steel lids over the chars to restrict oxygen entry from above. A few minutes later, with no flames left, I remove the lids, dig a quick hole in the centre of the char, tip in about a gallon of water and re-cover with the lids. The steam can now spread through the black char for about ten minutes, further breaking down its internal structure and increasing its surface area.

Finally, I use rainwater to douse the char and wash any ash through. I follow this by stirring and re-wetting to ensure there are no glowing embers left to re-ignite. Even the smallest pocket of glowing char will gradually expand and turn your stock to ash if it gets hold of the slightest amount of oxygen... Beware.

A steaming, open pit char, then covered to retain the steam.

CHAPTER 9, ADDING KILNS OR RETORTS INTO THE FIREPIT

The Flexi-Tubes or kilns should be introduced when the top of the fire is very hot with a curtain of flames rising from the feedstock and plenty of glowing secondary feedstock at the bottom of the barrel.

Try to position the kilns or retorts so that flames can lick around them evenly. Plug the tubes with soil at either end; otherwise the wood chips inside will catch fire. The loose capping soil allows decomposition gases to escape and be burned off, and this soil will also be sterilised by the heat, for use later to make a superb (and free) sterile seed compost. Simply mix it with finely crushed and charged BSM biochar.

The Flexi-Tubes may need occasional re-positioning in the firepit to ensure even temperatures around them or when building up the fire with more secondary feedstock. Always wear heat resistant gauntlets with no bare skin on show. sticking fork tines into the end is a good way to move flexi-Tubes.

The following illustration shows the end of a tube that is not sufficiently surrounded by flames and, therefore needs to be re-positioned and the fire made up.

After some time at a high heat, the soil will noticeably shrink down the tubes as the primary feedstock is decomposed to a fraction of its original volume. After the white smoke of moisture evaporation, comes yellowy and finally thin grey or blue smoke as volatiles are released during the thermal decomposition of the primary feedstock inside the Flexi-Tubes.

Next, combustible gases appear at the ends of each tube (see illustration below). These must be ignited in the swirling firepit to prevent methane from being released into the atmosphere. The gas flames will also add to the heat of the fire until it eventually dies down, which signifies that the biochar is nearly ready.

Towards the end of the process (after half an hour

to one and a half hours, depending on temperature, feedstock size and kiln diameter), add a small amount of water to each Flexi-Tube. This creates steam, improving the char's quality (allow five to ten minutes of steaming).

After removing the Flexi-Tubes from the flames by inserting fork tines into the open tube and wearing heat-proof gauntlets, let them cool naturally or douse them with more water before emptying. If the biochar is not fully cool, it might ignite as you admit oxygen to the char.

Reduced retort or kiln biochar after pyrolysis.

By the time the Flexi-Tubes have cooled and been emptied, the last of the secondary feedstock that was added to the firepit should have started to ash, and any smoke will be noticeably reduced or stopped. Break the final embers down into the lower part of the firepit and allow them to thermally decompose. I sometimes sit a loose steel lid on top of the coals at this point, to restrict the oxygen available.

Quench the coals in the centre, at the very bottom of the firepit with a small amount of water to steam the char (first make a hole in the char with a spade). When the firepit is steaming well, add a flat steel plate on top to hold in the steam.

After ten or fifteen minutes, douse the firepit thoroughly with rainwater to extinguish the char and wash through any ash from the process. Loosen the char with a fork and re-douse any hot spots. Do not leave ANY glowing embers.

CHAPTER 10 MONITORING FLEXI-TUBE PYROLYSIS

During pyrolysis, keep feeding the fire around the Flexi-Tube, high in the drum, so a vortex or curtain of fire surrounds the kilns. Now is the time to measure the temperature; firstly, the kiln's outer surface is measured using a digital laser thermometer, and then inside the tube, by pointing the laser onto the surface of the primary feedstock or soil plug. the picture below shows a typical external temperature.

My best biochar is produced in the temperature

range of 500-600 degrees centigrade, but the decomposition of the feedstock starts at a much lower temperature. First, water evaporates (white smoke), and then yellowy smoke is emitted as the feedstock decomposes. This is followed , after about half an hour, by thin blue smoke or none.

Remember, the drier the initial feedstock, the quicker the pyrolysis will occur.

Usually, towards the end, the feedstock gives off volatile gases such as methane, which can be seen burning inside the firepit. When the off-gassing has completely finished, the flames from the tops of the Flexi-Tubes will go out, signalling that pyrolysis has nearly stopped (allow a little longer to be sure) and the char in the tubes is ready for a period of steaming. Also, the feedstock will have shrunk down the tubes, almost out of sight (perhaps to a quarter the volume of the starter feedstock), but this is dependant on initial moisture content, feedstock particle size and how tightly the kiln was packed.

CHAPTER 11 KILN OR RETORT PYROLYSIS.

As decomposition occurs inside tin kilns or flexi-tubes, there will be smoke, visibly being emitted from the puncture holes or tube ends, then flames as methane is given off and ignited by the surrounding fire. Tiny flame jets will be apparent, shooting from the pierced tin kilns.

I have found with small batch pyrolysis, that the diameter of any vessel used as kilns should be a maximum of six inches so that good heat penetration can occur. It is a matter of trial and error, however, and if you get things wrong, partial pyrolysis will result, with some of the char looking patchy brown in colour rather than jet black, as below.

Properly finished char will be around one-quarter of the feedstock's original volume and another test, which demonstrates that adequate temperature was maintained, is that char dust will be easily rinsed from your hands with plain water (no soap needed). This shows that the volatiles like tar and oils have been driven off. Your raw, small batch char is now ready to be charged with nutrients and/or inoculated with microbes to make Black Soil Magic, completing the garden BSM biochar process. OR... some of the larger chunks may be used as a hot burning and easy to light barbecue fuel.

CHAPTER 12 SORTING THE FIREPIT CHAR

White or grey ash in the firepit signifies the parts of the secondary feedstock that burned in the presence of oxygen, whilst any remaining black char has partially decomposed under the effect of intense heat to leave almost pure, inert carbon.

With the firepit extinguished and cool, it is time to remove the raw char that has come from the secondary feedstock. If your steel drum has no bottom, it is easiest to tip and roll it away for access to the char with a shovel or spade, but before doing this, I remove any large lumps for later use as free barbeque charcoal. I chop the remaining stock into smaller pieces with a spade and shovel the char into a suitable vessel, trying to avoid the ash patches in the bottom of the firepit.

Ash is best kept separate from the char as it is usually more alkaline. Stored ash can be used to reduce soil acidity. It is about half as good as adding lime and contains many nutrients.

Raw char is often slightly alkaline, but it depends on the feedstock. It can be acidified using citrus tea, sulphur, Epsom salts, etc.

CHAPTER 13 CRUSHING THE CHAR

Although some chopping with a spade may have reduced the char, it is best crushed to pea size or less for use as a soil or compost amendment. The way that I achieve this is to run an old lawnmower over the wet char on a solid, flat surface. I lower the mower skirt to keep the char crumbs under the hood until flicked into the grass box. The char must be wet to reduce dust and the likelihood of re-ignition!

How and why should BSM be crushed?

Since experimenting with BSM biochar as a soil amendment in my allotment, I have discovered that a small particle size (pea size and below) offers the best results. Pea-sized bits open heavy soil and finer particles mix effortlessly to create an excellent dark tilth with a huge surface area for storing nutrients, air and water, while providing a good home for fungi, and microbes..

Char after crushing by the mower and my dirty hands, rinsed clean in rainwater, showing that no oily volatiles remain after thermal decomposition at the right temperature.

Larger pieces of char can be hydrophobic to begin with and if left on the soil surface, may stay that way for longer. Crushing before nutrient activation maximises the available surface area and reduces these hydrophobic tendencies.

A lump of char, shown still afloat after several days in a barrel. This demonstrates that crushing char before charging and adding to the garden is best because large pieces may be hydrophobic, initially.

CHAPTER 14 ACTIVATING OR CHARGING THE CHAR

I mostly nutrify the crushed char by adding it to my compost heap or mixing it with liquid fertiliser/weed tea for a week to two months. It may then be used as a soil amendment.

Once nutrified, the char can be inoculated with microbes by adding a handful of woodland soil, a small amount of manure, citrus tea, etc. After that, it can be termed BSM biochar in the full sense of the word.

Crushed wet char

It is important to note that char is relatively inert after initial production and MUST, therefore, be activated or charged with a suitable balance of nutrients or inoculated with beneficial microbes for maximum effect. Failure to do so before adding to soil may lead to the possibility that the raw (empty) char soaks up all available nutrients, temporarily depriving your plants of access to them, which is of no benefit.

One of the best ways to charge raw char is in the compost heap. Here, it acts as an activator, effectively retaining water or air and adsorbing the nutrients of decay. Alternatively, nutrification may be achieved by soaking the char in weed-liquid fertiliser for a few days.

Introducing BSM as an amendment will boost the cation exchange capacity (the ability to attract nutrients for plants to access), of your soil. This is particularly useful in sandy areas. Most often, BSM biochar will be alkaline, which will help neutralise acidic conditions and, in all soil types, it will provide a home in which microorganisms and fungi can thrive.

BSM biochar added to garden soil will also sequester (capture) carbon and reduce nutrient leaching. This may mean that over the growing season, fewer nutrients need to be applied to your crops to achieve better results.

Once added, BSM biochar remains without further decomposition in soil for hundreds or thousands of years (unlike manure/compost, which slowly breaks down).

CHAPTER 15 WHY IS BSM SO GOOD?

It has been established, but is worth reiterating, that biochar, or Black Soil Magic as I love to call it, is a long-lasting, carbon-rich soil amendment that enhances plant growth, vigour and connectivity, increasing plant disease resistance. This comes about because BSM biochar acts like a sponge, providing a valuable habitat for nutrients, soil microbes and fungi and enhancing their connectivity with a plant's rhizosphere (root system). In turn, this further reduces leaching into watercourses and enhances the soil's cation exchange capacity (nutrient transfer capability). Once charged, char can be introduced to the soil as a beneficial amendment, particularly helpful in structurally poor or acidic conditions.

The amendment of poor or acidic allotment soil with nutrified and inoculated Biochar (Black Soil Magic) and/or homemade compost/weed-feed liquid, helps ensure lush crops with minimal dependence on artificial fertilisers.

Reduced leaching, improved drought tolerance and better disease resistance due to the enhanced soil community (biome) are the most noticeable improvements in poor soil types, but Black Soil

Magic can benefit every allotment garden, whatever its initial state. One easy way to see change comes from the darkening of topsoil, which increases absorption of the sun's rays (and warmth). The higher cation exchange capacity in the soil is more challenging to spot, but rest assured, with BSM biochar added to your soil, any positives will remain for hundreds of years.

Charcoal produced for fuel is heated to 200-300 degrees Celsius, but BSM biochar for soil amendment is thermally decomposed at higher temperatures (300, to 1000 centigrade in rapid production systems). These ultra-high temperatures break down plant lignin and cellulose and remove other compounds, making the end product crumbly, with a larger available surface area for adsorption and more micropores. A higher cation exchange capacity is a typical attribute of this char.

Not only is BSM biochar a valuable addition to the garden, but by decomposing your organic matter at low oxygen levels, less CO_2 is released into the atmosphere. This is because the carbon within char becomes sequestered (captured) and is removed from the carbon cycle for hundreds of years. Particularly useful in these environmentally challenged times.

Here in the UK, with ever-increasing rainfall due to climate change, lower nutrient leaching from allotment or garden soils can reduce pollution in rivers, lakes, and streams. It also means a lower fertiliser application rate will achieve the same production level, making plant growth more efficient and less costly.

The quality and quantity of finished BSM biochar depend on feedstock, pyrolysis conditions, and pre- or post-pyrolysis treatments. However, Black Soil Magic (biochar) will have positive effects on most soils.

One example centres on the fact that potassium in soil is particularly susceptible to leaching. Because biochar increases the CEC (cation exchange capacity), it strengthens potassium retention. Also, Biochar's ability to form humus by encouraging fungal communities to thrive can only be seen as a positive in any leaching-susceptible soils.

BSM biochar also encourages increased biological nitrogen fixation, especially in sandy and acidic soils. This, in itself, offers improved N retention by leguminous plants, which can benefit other crops afterwards.

Biochar's role in enhancing soil microbial activity and raising PH prevents phosphate fixation in acidic soils and increases its solubilisation, thus increasing soil phosphorous availability.

Knowledge of the most appropriate ways to prepare and apply BSM biochar for soil amendment is essential if the product is to be used effectively. However, a try-it-out approach can cause few unexpected downsides on an allotment scale. Likewise, small-scale production of chars is low-tech. Therefore, an experimental approach is likely to yield beneficial results as long as the char elements of fire are recognised and separated from the ash component to establish a useful product.

The current retail price of biochar soil amendment products means making your own BSM biochar can be a significant cost saver. Don't forget that a bonus batch, for use as lump wood charcoal, means the family can enjoy free allotment or garden barbecues all year round.

When describing BSM biochar as a soil amendment, I have likened it to a rechargeable battery. In equivalent terms, garden compost is a standard battery. Once depleted, the standard battery cannot be re-energised, unlike the rechargeable one. Because of this, it is only necessary to make enough BSM biochar to service your needs. Compost acts similarly to char, however, because it continues to decay in the soil, it needs more to be made all of the time.

But, exactly why is turning organic waste into BSM Biochar better for the Eco-System than composting or burning it?

Creating biochar reduces CO2 in the atmosphere because it takes the carbon-neutral process of naturally decaying organic matter and turns it carbon-negative: When plants decay, they emit CO2, which other plants absorb, and the cycle continues. Biochar stabilises that decaying matter and puts it in the ground for hundreds or thousands of years, preventing further CO2 release. This idea has enormous potential to help slow global warming, while simultaneously helping with the sustainable regeneration of soils across the world.

CHAPTER 16   BSM APPLICATION RATES

BSM biochar, when crushed to pea size or below and charged with nutrients (mixed with compost or soaked in liquid fertiliser), can be added to soil at rates of up to fifteen litres per metre squared (ten per cent by volume).

When adding raw char to activate early-stage compost piles, enhance microbial activity and optimise the carbon/nitrogen ratio, a 1-5 ratio by volume is acceptable. Allow several weeks or months before applying the end product to the soil (depending on temperature).

An alternative way to charge the raw char involves steeping in liquid fertiliser for a few days. After this activation, up to twenty per cent addition of BSM biochar to mature compost, yields good results.

There is no definitive answer to application rates, the above being guides. For example, if your soil is very acidic, a higher amount of BSM can have a positive effect, whereas, alkaline soils may suit lower applications unless measures are taken to subsequently correct the soil PH.

CHAPTER 17   OTHER USES FOR THE FIREPIT AND THE CHAR

Sterilising small quantities of garden soil and compost over a fire is an easy and cheap way to provide a pest and disease-free seed starting medium. This will minimise the environmental footprint of allotment or any form of gardening and save money.

A more minor positive of biochar production where the householder is concerned is that a portion of DIY-produced char may be burned like charcoal, providing a further cost saving (when dried for use as barbeque fuel).

Chunky dry char for barbecue use.

Homemade biochar is a low-cost, eco-friendly amendment that enhances the soil or compost microbiome, but did you know it can be crushed and placed inside socks to deodourise shoes or used to make toothpaste? Other roles include cat litter tray deodoriser.

The smoke from biochar production can be condensed into wood vinegar (acetic acid, acetone and methanol), which has a low PH (2-3) and is a valuable natural bio-stimulant and horticultural pesticide, e.g. it is suitable for controlling flea beetle. Dilute one part with fifty parts of water for sprinkling on the compost pile or with 200 parts of water before adding to the soil at one litre per square metre.

Using firepits, kilns and retorts to create sterile seed compost in the self-contained allotment garden.

A garden firepit, kiln or retort is handy for most gardens and essential if you wish to make good biochar. BSM will drive long-term humus formation, which is well worth the effort. After soaking char in liquid fertiliser to make Black Soil Magic, adding up to twenty per cent by volume will regenerate spent compost, saving pounds per year. Heat is the key here. We must eliminate soil-borne pests, diseases or harmful fungi in the spent compost that might ruin your seedlings. Remember, char is sterilised during pyrolysis, and part of the heat from this process can be used to sterilise small batches of garden soil or compost inside DIY kilns or retorts.

Blending various concentrations of these sterilised ingredients will provide a good starter or follow-on growth medium, ensuring a solid plant start, with good root growth and this regenerated product can be sieved to suit your needs.

CHAPTER 18   COMPOSTING WITH BSM BIOCHAR.

Composting

Composting converts plant and animal waste into a balanced, humus-rich, nutrient-dense garden additive by decay in the presence of microbial action. Initially, the waste requires some nutrients, especially nitrogen to feed the process, but soon a surplus exists and from then on, the product may be used to feed your plant's growth whilst continuing to decompose. Eventually, it will become humus, with most of its nutrients discharged, but in this state it finds a useful equilibrium in hosting soil fungi and microbes to benefit plant growth further.

The composting process relies on a mix of ingredients in suitable ratios. Most plants are made from two main elements, carbon and nitrogen, and others in smaller quantities.

The key factors to get right when compost-making are:

Maintain an overall ratio of around 35:1 carbon to nitrogen from the ingredients mixture.

Ensure the presence of enough moisture. The pile should not be soaking wet; it should just be damp for the duration.

Create small particle sizes by breaking up the different ingredients to allow better mixing.

Introduce and maintain air within the pile. If you do not want anaerobic conditions to develop with foul smells, etc, turn the heap at least once or more to introduce fresh air.

Size of heap... If hot composting is required (which speeds up the entire process), the heap must be big enough to retain the generated heat (about three feet cubed is about right in the UK.) This heat kills weed seeds and perennial roots. Creating compost without noticeable heat is possible, but it takes longer.

The Carbon to Nitrogen Ratio

Understanding various compost ingredients' carbon-to-nitrogen ratio (some people call it the green-to-brown ratio) helps manage your pile. For example, chicken manure has a ratio of about 7:1, grass clippings 20:1, paper/cardboard about 130:1 and woodchips 500:1. Biochar is almost pure carbon and dependent on the feedstock is unlikely to contain inherent nitrogen, so has a very high ratio indeed. However, in its inert state, vast pore spaces and the colossal surface area within which microbes, nutrients, moisture and air can be harboured, make char a valuable catalyst in the decay process even if only a small amount is added. I add up to twenty per cent, depending on how far the compost heap is along the road to decomposition (a higher proportion of char can be added to a more finished compost).

As we are trying to achieve around a 35:1 carbon to nitrogen ratio overall, too many wood chips (500:1), could be less than ideal. It is also important to note that, when the wood content is large and solid, getting a balanced mixture of carbon and nitrogen will be impossible. In one example, using freshly mown grass and wood chips as your only ingredients means a lot more grass than wood is required in your heap. However, too much grass or poor mixing usually creates a slimy mess (mixing in finely crushed biochar helps avoid this). Adjustments should be made by keeping an eye on the pile. If there is no heat, add greens (below a 30:1 ratio), or when the heap becomes smelly, add more browns (plant matter over 30:1 ratio).

Humus

As compost decomposes, it creates a small amount of stable, soil organic matter (humus), which can survive in the soil for decades. Compost can take a hundred years to break down to humus, a loose, spongy and crumbly reservoir for nutrients, microbes and fungi. While being converted, it feeds your plants gradually and supports the soil biome.

In a way, biochar is similar to or could even be described as humus. This is because it represents the end of the decomposition process and can only act as a reservoir for nutrients, microbes and fungi. The difference is that biochar has reached its humus state almost instantly during pyrolysis. BSM biochar powers the soil after being charged with nutrients, microbes and fungi. It may be replenished with more nutrients like a rechargeable battery, continuing to cycle for a thousand years.

The fantastic properties of BSM biochar (including alkalinity) must be considered when comparing historically made compost (without biochar added) and compost that includes BSM biochar (pre-charged with specific nutrients and microbes). Each of these products may have different benefits and applications.

*Some people use the words humus-rich to describe soil with organic matter in the process of turning into humus, either by decomposition or the action of worms, slugs, microorganisms, etc. Technically, though, humus is the end product.

SUMMARY AND CONCLUSION

DIY BSM biochar production is a must for all gardens, allotments and small holdings. It is a fabulously exciting (but not new) idea, achieved by subjecting any formerly living thing to pyrolysis (thermal decomposition in a reduced oxygen environment), to create a long-term, useful product, while simultaneously achieving carbon capture for the benefit of the planet...

The char can be made for free, on a small scale at the allotment, in the garden or on a small holding. Each batch will deliver a long-lasting, carbon-rich structure, with just a few grams having the surface area of several tennis courts. The vast pore spaces within and around the char edges may be charged with nutrients and inoculated with microbes to become active BSM biochar, ready to add to your soil.

While growing, plants gradually deplete the supply of nutrients in BSM biochar, but the char can be re-energised repeatedly like a rechargeable battery.

Because Black Soil Magic (biochar) anchors nutrients close to roots in the soil, it reduces leaching while those nutrients remain plant-available.

Furthermore, BSM (Black Soil Magic) provides a fantastic home where microbes, microorganisms, and fungi flourish.

BSM simultaneously removes carbon from the carbon cycle, reducing CO2 emissions for hundreds of years.

Although biochar needs only to be made once, I believe that any self-contained allotment holders trying it out will be hooked on production from then on. It is a joyous fact that even the most noxious weed roots, such as bindweed, couch, brambles and nettles, can successfully be turned into biochar, meaning those old adversaries can become firm allotment or garden friends.

Now that you have made biochar, it is time to conduct your own experiments to test the results on your land.

Please take a look at the following recipe for making your own Black Soil Magic by mixing weed nutrient liquid, compost and char.

BLACK SOIL MAGIC (BSM)... A WEEDCHAR AND COMPOST RECIPE:

Produce a multi-purpose BSM compost enriched with char and weed-liquid nutrient extract.

Ready in **5 weeks to 5 months (depending on temperature)**

Benefits: **Biochar aids the composting process by providing air spaces and a home for microbes, moisture and nutrients within the compost. It will also remain in the soil longer than other forms**

of organic matter and has a vast surface area for adsorbing nutrients, acting like a rechargeable battery.

In the nutrient weed liquid, green leaves add nitrogen and potassium, while weed roots/tea add phosphorus to provide a balanced supply of nutrients or adjust as necessary for specific needs.

***This recipe adds char at the beginning of the composting process; hence, a lower proportion of char is used than when adding char to finished compost.**

Ingredients

- A mix of crushed and lumpy char(pea-sized) wetted with non-chlorinated water or nutrient weed liquid.

- Non-seeded grass clippings or similar high-nitrogen green leaves.

- A few handfuls of woodland soil to innoculate the mixture with microbes

- A small quantity of granulated sugar to boost the action.

- A nutrient liquid from fermented or , noxious weeds and their roots or seeds.

- Nettle leaves and stems (not if seeding, and wear gloves to pick).

- Comfrey leaves (wear gloves to pick).

Preparation

1. **Add the weeds to a vat of rainwater and leave to rot or ferment for a few months, then drain the nutrient liquid.**
2. **Mix the green ingredients thoroughly with char (up to ten per cent by volume), infused with weed-nutrient liquid.**
3. **Turn every week to aerate, and add a little sugar to feed the microbes.**
4. **Ready from five weeks to five months (dependent on temperature).**

Tips

If the pile becomes smelly, add slightly more char; if it falls below fifty per cent moisture, add water or weed-nutrient liquid.

The result will be a nutritious weedchar compost that benefits soil and plants.

The BSM biochar element will remain in your soil to be repeatedly recharged with fresh nutrients.

Leaching will be reduced for hundreds of years, meaning less nutrients need to be applied to your crops.

Soil will become darker in colour, thus absorbing sunlight better (warming up earlier).

The soil PH may be raised, so do not over-apply, especially to already alkaline soil.

* Always test your soil and if the mixture becomes too alkaline, add sulphur or Epsom salts (magnesium sulphate).

**For fun, here is a random picture of a tree
serpent. spotted out on an autumn walk
in the Lincolnshire countryside.**

Crushing char the hard way, by hand.

Baked bean can pyrolysis, partially incomplete.

Bindweed roots make a satisfying feedstock